SPORTS FROM COAST TO COAST™

WATER POLO
RULES, TIPS, STRATEGY, AND SAFETY

—— TRACIE EGAN ——

rosen
central™

The Rosen Publishing Group, Inc.,
New York

Published in 2005 by The Rosen Publishing Group, Inc.
29 East 21st Street, New York, NY 10010

Library of Congress Cataloging-in-Publication Data

Egan, Tracie.
Water polo: rules, tips, strategy, and safety / by Tracie Egan.—1st ed.
    p. cm.—(Sports from coast to coast)
Includes bibliographical references and index.
ISBN 1-4042-0186-6 (library binding)
1. Water polo—Juvenile literature. [1. Water polo.] I. Title. II. Series.
GV839.E43 2004
797.2'5—dc22

                                                    2003023671

Manufactured in the United States of America

CONTENTS

CHAPTER ONE

The History of Water Polo

William Wilson revived interest in swimming races in the 1870s by making the races a form of "water soccer."

When you consider that many sports have been played for hundreds or even thousands of years, the game of water polo is relatively young. Little is known about the origin of the sport, but it is believed that a Scotsman named William Wilson helped to create water polo in the 1870s. At this time in Great Britain, swimming races were declining in popularity because spectators were becoming bored with the repetitive nature of the sport. It is not as interesting for an audience to watch individuals compete against time as it is to watch people compete against each other. Swimming clubs in Great Britain began playing a version of "water soccer" in lakes and rivers, even though man-made swimming pools were in existence and were popular by this time. In 1876, at the request of the swimming club he belonged to in Scotland, Wilson drew up a list of rules for the game. The version that Wilson created was not quite like today's game, but it involved elements of tag, diving, and soccer, just like the modern version of water polo.

The game wasn't considered a significant sport at first. Originally, it was thought of as entertainment for audiences attending swimming competitions or for people at seaside resorts. But eventually, people began to see the potential in water polo as a popular sport, and they began working to refine the game.

There's a great deal of debate among sports historians over where the name "water polo" comes from. Some people believe that the name is derived from another game known as water derby. Water derby was being played as entertainment for spectators at swimming events as well. In this game, men would mount barrels as if they were riding a horse, and often the name of a well-known racehorse would be painted along the side of the barrel. The object of the game was to knock people off the barrels while a hockey-style game was played on the surface of the water. The similarity between the game of polo that's played with real horses and water derby led people to call it aquatic polo or water polo. Water derby never evolved past a simple entertainment, but the name stuck to the game that William Wilson had developed.

The term "polo" may have been applied to this sport because of the type of ball, an Indian rubber ball, that was used in early versions of the game. *Pulu* is the Hindi word for ball, but it was mispronounced by the English as "polo." This second theory is probably more accurate, as there is no documentation of water derby other than some illustrations by artists who had never even played the game.

Early water polo games were nothing more than a type of aquatic wrestling and demonstrations of a player's strength. There weren't really positions, and the only offensive strategy used was that each player just try to score a goal every chance he or she could get. The more water polo was played, the more thought people put into the rules so that it could be considered a serious sport. In the 1880s, water polo really began to take off, and most of the rules were created within that decade. The rules that were implemented moved the style of play away from rugby and closer to soccer, with the game being less about brute strength and more about speed and technique. The time of play was established, as was the size of the goal cages. A leather soccer ball replaced the small rubber pulu. The invention of the Trudgeon stroke helped revolutionize the game. The Trudgeon stroke, a swimming technique, allowed for a faster moving game that was centered a bit more around swimming. In 1888, A. Sinclair, the founder of the London Water Polo League, put together a committee to formalize the rules and

Most of the rules for water polo were created in the 1880s so that the game could become a serious sport. The first water polo leagues were formed in Great Britain.

HOUNSLOW PREMIER S.C. POLO TEAM.

WINNERS OF THE

MIDDLESEX JUNIOR QUALIFYING COMPETITION, 1911.

R. A. WHITTINGTON   W. J. HEWETT (*Vice-Captain*).   J. DAVEY

F. MILLER   C. E. WHITTINGTON   S. A. BROWN   R. SARGEANT

S. WHITTINGTON (*Captain*).

Members of an early-twentieth-century women's water polo team pose with their league award. The first women's water polo match was held in 1906, but the first Olympic women's water polo competition was not held until 2000.

to add more structure to the game. What the committee came up with was a set of rules that are very similar to those that are used today. In 1891, the game reached an important milestone. That year, England's two most prestigious universities, Oxford and Cambridge, played their first varsity water polo match.

Around that time, word of the sport spread to America through Englishman John Robinson, a professional swimming instructor who worked at the Boston Athletic Association. Because Robinson was working in America at the time that A. Sinclair's water polo committee was changing the rules of the sport, Robinson was unaware of those changes and introduced the rugby style of water polo. Rugby is vaguely similar to American football, which is one of the most popular sports in the United States. The American game took on a football feel. This version of water polo, known as "American style," became a huge hit in the United States. Within ten years, the sport was played in major arenas like Madison Square Garden and attracted as many as 15,000 spectators during national championships.

In February 1891, the first published rules for American-style water polo appeared in *Harper's Weekly* magazine. Much like the

Water Football

All around the world, the game that Americans call "soccer" is actually called "football." While water polo was still in its early stages of development, the English referred to it as water football. Those words meant something very different to American athletes, which may have contributed to the early differences between the American and English versions of water polo.

American water polo is now played like soccer, as it is in England. But at first, the American version was a lot like rugby, which is similar to American football.

evolution of the game in England, the early American-style water polo differed greatly from the version of the sport that is played today in the United States. In the beginning, American-style water polo was one of the most dangerous sports ever played. Just about any move was legal, including holding another player underwater for long periods of time. In fact, the intensity of the play and the violence of the game is what attracted most spectators to the sport at the time. As water polo spread across the United States, more teams and leagues were developed. Eventually, the "soccer style" of playing water polo, known then as the "English rules" game, was adopted by U.S. teams.

While water polo was being introduced in the United States, it was spreading quickly throughout Europe as an exciting new sport, with leagues being formed first in France, Germany, and Belgium, and eventually all over the continent. In 1900, the sport of water polo was widespread enough to be added to the program of the Olympic Games. In fact, water polo was the first team sport to be added to the Olympic program, leading the way for many other sports. The 1900 Olympic Games were played in Paris, France. Because travel abroad was so expensive and because the Olympic version of water polo would be played according to "English rules," the Olympic water polo tournament did not at first attract Americans.

In 1929, an international water polo board was formed. It consisted of four representatives from England and four representatives from the Fédération Internationale de Natation Amateur (FINA), the

A page from a late-nineteenth-century *Harper's Weekly* magazine shows illustrations of several highlights during a water polo match.

This Hungarian men's water polo team took the Olympic gold medal in 1936. During its early stages, water polo was seen only as a men's game.

worldwide water sports organization founded in 1908. At first, it was basically a British organization, but it has since developed into an organization that represents all parts of the world. All water polo matches are now played under the rules defined by FINA.

During the development of water polo, it was strictly a men's game. Water polo was believed to be too rigorous for a proper young lady, not to mention that bathing suits, although quite modest in those days, were thought to be far too revealing for them. But more and more women around the world were becoming suffragists, advocating for the vote and demanding equality in all activities. It was inevitable that women would also want to get in on the fun and exercise of team sports like water polo. The first documented women's water polo match was held in Holland in 1906.

In 1911, New York's National Women's Lifesaving League formed a swimming and water polo league. A woman named Charlotte Epstein, a legal stenographer from the New York area, was the main organizer of the league, as well as the founder of the Women's Swimming Association (WSA). Epstein's vision for introducing women to the sport of water polo was to instill confidence,

Charlotte Epstein founded the Women's Swimming Association in 1917 so that she and a few other businesswomen could swim after work. The WSA promoted the health benefits of water polo to women.

to teach lifesaving skills, to develop strength, and, perhaps most important, to just have fun. The first FINA Women's Water Polo World Cup was held in 1979, but it wasn't until 2000 that women's water polo was played in the Olympic Games—exactly 100 years after the men's.

CHAPTER TWO

Equipment and Techniques

In water polo, the players wear numbered and color-coded swimming caps to make it easy to tell which team they're on.

Water polo does not require the use of that much equipment, as it is difficult enough to tread water while playing a game with a ball. But the equipment that is required for an official water polo game is divided into two categories: playing equipment (used by the players) and officiating equipment (used by the referees and secretaries).

Playing Equipment

Because the players are immersed in water up to their necks, it's difficult to tell one player from another, or even which team they belong to, by the colors or patterns of their bathing suits. Therefore, players are required to wear swimming caps that are numbered. One team wears light-colored caps, while the other team wears a dark color. Each goalie is assigned the number 1 and required to wear a red cap.

The water polo ball has evolved over the years, but the ball used in games today is very similar to a soccer ball. It is round, and it must be fully inflated. If the ball is not fully inflated, it has the potential to be hazardous, as it will bounce swiftly off the water. The circumference measures between 25 and 28 inches (between 0.6 and 0.7 meters). It weighs between 14 and 16 ounces (between 400 and 450 grams).

The pool that a water polo game is played in is generally 82 feet by 66 feet (26 m by 20 m). It should be between 6.5 and 26 feet (2 and 8 m) deep—the deeper the better. Players are supposed to tread water, not walk on the bottom of the pool. The pool is divided into sections, similar to those of a soccer field. There is a center line dividing the pool into two halves. Each half has lines measuring out from the front of the goal. There is one goal box at each end of the pool. The goals are 10 feet (3 m) wide and are made of either wood or metal. Nets are attached to the goal in order to catch the ball.

Officiating Equipment

The rules of water polo define a number of fouls and penalties, so the most important piece of equipment that a referee possesses is his or

A water polo referee signals a foul by blowing a whistle and making a hand signal. Fouls are an important part of this game's strategy. There are three types of fouls in water polo: ordinary, exclusion, and penalty.

her whistle. While the referees and goal judge use hand signals to signify a different call, the game secretaries may use a flag to indicate the expiration of foul periods and game reentry of players.

Water polo borrows aspects of many other sports, so it's not surprising that the timekeeping resembles that of basketball. There are two clocks used for a game of water polo, as in basketball. One clock indicates the time remaining in a quarter, while the other, called the shot clock, indicates how much time remains for the offense to shoot the ball into the goal.

The techniques of playing water polo are just as important as the rules. Many skills are required of a player, the most obvious one being swimming ability. Because swimming uses every muscle in the body and is extremely exhausting, an athlete must be in top shape to swim or tread water for an entire game of water polo. The best swimming

A regulation water polo pool is divided in half by a center line. It is also divided into smaller sections like a soccer field. The deeper the pool the better, as the players must tread water at all times during the game.

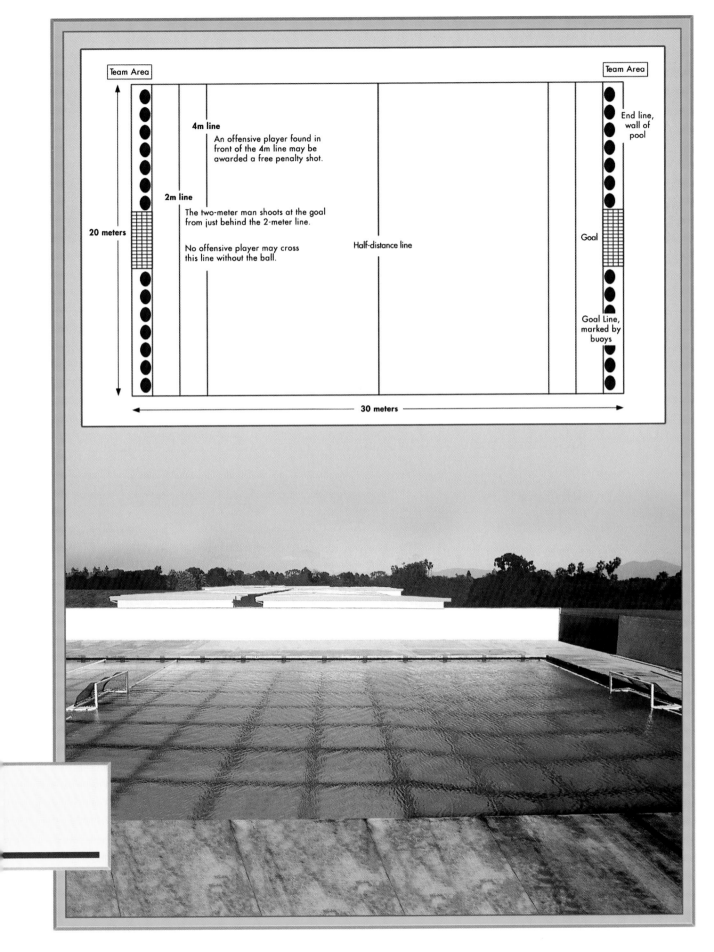

Team Area

Team Area

20 meters

4m line

An offensive player found in front of the 4m line may be awarded a free penalty shot.

2m line

The two-meter man shoots at the goal from just behind the 2-meter line.

No offensive player may cross this line without the ball.

Half-distance line

End line, wall of pool

Goal

Goal Line, marked by buoys

30 meters

position for the game is, obviously, one where the player can see what is going on. This means that players do not use the usual competitive swimming style, with the body as horizontal as possible and the head in the water. Instead, a style akin to that used by lifeguards, with the head out of the water, is used.

Treading water is another important skill in water polo, and it is vital to catching, passing, or shooting the ball. While treading water, the player is in a vertical (upright) position, with the head and preferably the shoulders above the water. The legs are constantly kicking in what's known as an eggbeater kick, where the legs move alternately, resembling a kitchen eggbeater. The arms are used to maintain balance, but when the arms are needed for handling the ball, the legs are required to work overtime in order for the player's body to maintain a vertical position.

Swimming and treading water are the most basic skills required of a water polo player. But in order to score goals, it is necessary for a player to be a competent ball handler. The best handlers hold the ball with as little tension as possible. When holding the ball, it is partially in the palm and partially on the fingers, but never in the flat of the hand. The fingers must remain relaxed, while the arm remains bent, forming a right angle at the elbow. When throwing the ball, the arm rotates, drawing the ball back. The ball is held high from the surface of the water. The arm then swings forward, while the body faces the spot that the player intends to pass to. The legs should still be "egg beating" while the free arm is maintaining balance.

Endurance is key to being a successful water polo player. As players battle for the ball, try to score goals, and play defense, they must be swimming the entire time. The top water polo players are among the best-conditioned athletes in the world.

Controlling the ball while swimming is quite a difficult task. It is important for the player to adhere to established techniques in order to be a better handler and dribbler. In water polo, dribbling is when a player swims with the ball. This is achieved through a "crawl" stroke, where the player moves forward in the water with his or her head up, while stroking with the arms. The ball is carried in the wave created by the chest. As the player moves forward, the ball will move with the wave. To change directions when dribbling, the player can nudge the ball with the inside of his or her arms while turning the body.

In water polo, there are "wet" passes and "dry" passes. Wet passes are when the ball hits the water first before reaching one's teammate. Dry passes are when the ball is passed directly from player to player. It is much more difficult to successfully execute a dry pass, as it is difficult enough to tread water and see everything going on during the game. Most passes made are wet passes because they are easier to manage. A wet pass, if properly executed, tends to put the ball in the water right in front of your teammate. A dry pass may require your teammate to rise out of the water at just the right moment to catch the ball.

Passing the ball to other players is important for victory, but games could not be won without the skill of shot-taking. Many players view shooting as the most important technique, but it's also the skill that must be practiced most. A good eye and a strong wrist are crucial to mastering an accurate shot. There are a number of different kinds of shots that are taken on a goal. The lob shot, for

Moving the ball in water polo is similar to dribbling in basketball, except the ball floats on the water's surface. A player can lift the ball out of the water and pass or shoot it, but unless he or she is the goalkeeper, he or she cannot touch the ball with both hands at the same time or hit it with a fist.

Goalies are the only players allowed to touch the ball with both hands or punch it. They are not permitted to pass the half-distance line but are allowed to shoot at the opposing team's goal.

example, is a deceptive, high arching shot that is intended to pass over the goalie and under the crossbar of the goal. Another type of shot is the sling shot. It resembles that of a discus thrower: the ball is thrown with a straight arm with a low sweep over the water. Finally, the push shot is a straight forward, pushing maneuver that is meant to look like a natural swimming stroke. Each shot has its advantages and disadvantages, which makes them an important part of any practice drill.

Obviously, shooting, passing, and dribbling are the main techniques for offensive play in water polo. But the techniques of defensive play are just as important. The two major features of defensive play are marking and tackling. Both are used to break up the offense. Water polo is a contact sport, which means that the players physically interact with each other, using their bodies to block the ball or other players. Marking occurs when a defensive player chooses an offensive player to guard. Tackling occurs when a defensive player holds, pulls, or pushes down an offensive player, usually when the offensive player is holding the ball. Tackling is legal in water polo, as long as it is carried out in a manner that will not cause injury.

Defensive skills are also very important in water polo. Here, a player from one team marks, or guards, an opponent.

Of course, skill is a plus in any sport, but an athlete cannot rely solely on natural ability. Knowledge of the techniques of water polo will only improve a player's game, and practice makes perfect.

CHAPTER THREE

The Rules of the Game

Caps are a crucial part of the players' uniforms. If a cap is repeatedly lost or untied, the referee can temporarily stop the game.

Water polo can be a confusing game to watch if one is not familiar with the rules. The game is loud and fast paced, with a lot of motion and splashing. The whistle of the referee seems to always be in use, although game play remains continuous, even when a foul or penalty is called. For a game that was invented as a spectator sport, the constant action of water polo is important. So the rules have been devised with the audience in mind, to keep the action going.

The object of water polo, as with most ball sports, is to score points by getting the ball into the opponent's goal. The team with the most points at the end of the game is the victor. The ball is advanced on the court, or pool, by throwing it or swimming with it. One of the fundamental rules of water polo is that no player other than the goalie may use both hands at the same time when handling the ball. Players are also not permitted to strike a water polo ball with a closed fist, in the way that a volleyball player spikes a ball, although they are allowed to use other body parts to advance the ball or to take a shot on the goal.

A game of water polo is divided into four quarters, each quarter lasting seven minutes. As in basketball, when the offensive team is on the opponent's side of the pool, they have a limited amount of time to take a shot at the goal. A score does not have to occur, but a shot must be attempted. If a shot is not attempted in the thirty-five-second time period, the offense will lose possession of the ball.

There are lines marked on each half of the pool. Each line has its own purpose. The two-meter line is located two meters in front of the goal. The offensive team cannot pass this line unless they are holding the ball or if the ball is in front of them. The four-meter line is located four meters in front of the goal. If an offensive player is in possession of the ball and is fouled in the area between the goal and the four-meter line, he or she may be awarded a penalty shot. The seven-meter line is located seven meters in front of the goal. When a foul is committed against an offensive player beyond this line, the player may

take a free throw or a direct shot into the goal. The center line is what it sounds like—it is located in the center of the water polo field. At the start of each quarter, the ball is placed on the center line. Each team then races from its own goal line, swimming at top speed, to gain possession of the ball. This is known as the sprint. Whichever side the ball is then taken over to is called the strong side, while the side without the ball is called the weak side. After a goal is scored, the players take positions anywhere within their respective fields of play.

In many sports, fouls are considered a hindrance to play by both the offense and the defense, and are typically avoided. However, in water polo, as in basketball, fouls are part of an offensive team's strategy. The offense will typically try to get the defense to commit fouls because the free throws and penalty shots that can be awarded provide the best opportunity to score a goal.

There are three types of fouls in water polo: ordinary, exclusion, and penalty fouls. Ordinary fouls are called for minor offenses that include touching the ball with two hands, taking the ball underwater, wasting time, or obstructing an offensive player without the ball. Other ordinary fouls include pushing, failing to advance the ball, or failing to take a shot at the goal within the thirty-five-second time limit. When a referee calls an ordinary foul, possession of the ball is given over to the opposing team at the location of the foul. If an ordinary foul is called on the defense between the two-meter line and the

When a player tackles a member of the opposing team, he or she must be careful not to strike that player or use foul language. If he or she does so, the referee will call an exclusion foul and the player will have to sit out twenty seconds of the game.

A water polo game consists of four quarters of play, each a maximum of seven minutes long. The entire game consists of only twenty-eight minutes of play. For this reason, the rules are designed to keep the game going as continuously and as quickly as possible. Stalling, or wasting time, is a common reason for calling an ordinary foul.

goal, the offense is automatically awarded a free throw at the goal. The free throw must be taken within three seconds, and if the ball is not put into play within three seconds, possession of the ball is awarded to the defense.

Exclusion fouls are for more serious infractions, including kicking or striking an opponent with intent to injure, interfering with a free throw, splashing, and misconduct such as foul language, violent behavior, or disrespecting referees. When an exclusion foul is called, the opposing team is awarded a free throw, while the player who has committed the foul is temporarily removed from the game. The player must go to the reentry area, which is located near the team's bench at

When the referee calls an exclusion foul, the offending player must wait in the reentry area for twenty seconds of actual game play or until a point has been scored or possession of the ball changes. If a player fouls three times, he or she is removed from the game.

the side of the pool, and cannot return to the game until twenty seconds of actual game play has occurred, possession of the ball changes, or a goal has been scored. If a player commits three exclusion fouls in a game, he or she is removed from the game completely.

Since an exclusion foul leaves a team with one less player, goals are more easily scored by the opposing team. A popular strategy in water polo is to provoke a player of the opposing team into committing an exclusion foul, because attacking the goal with a one-man advantage will more likely result in a score. During an exclusion, a team will switch from marking into a zone defense. Zone defense is when a player guards an area of the water, rather than another player.

Penalty fouls are the most serious infractions. They are called when a defending player commits any foul that obstructs a likely score, when a defending player commits an act of brutality within the four-meter area, or when the coach of the team not in possession of the ball requests a time-out. When a penalty foul is called on a player, the opposing team is awarded a penalty throw. A penalty throw is a direct shot on the goal and is thrown by the person that the foul was committed against.

For each of these fouls—ordinary, exclusion, and penalty—the referee can award throws to the offense as he or she sees fit. There are several different types of throws, each with its own style and purpose. When a free throw is awarded to the offense, the defense may not block or interfere with the throw in any manner. If they do, another foul will be called. A corner throw is a kind of free throw awarded to the offense when the defense touches the ball before it crosses the defensive goal line, outside of the goalposts. The offensive team will then throw the ball back into play from the side of the two-meter line.

Holding the Ball

Unlike basketball, in water polo the player holding the ball cannot be fouled. A player is considered to be holding the ball if it is in his or her hand or if it is floating on the water with the player's hand on top of it. A player is not considered to be holding the ball if he or she is dribbling, that is, swimming with the ball cradled in the water near the chest. It is legal to grab, push, hold, or dunk the holder of the ball. This makes water polo a uniquely exciting game with an element of roughness resembling rugby.

Another type of throw is a neutral throw. This is also referred to as a face-off. Face-offs are awarded when two players, one from offense and one from defense, commit a foul at the same time. During a face-off, the referee will blow his or her whistle and drop the ball between the players.

Aside from being removed from the game by an exclusion foul, the only time a player is permitted to leave the water is during an interval, or time between quarters, or when a referee gives a player permission (usually in the case of an emergency). A substitute may then be allowed to enter the game.

The Referee

A water polo referee's job is a hard one. The game is quick moving, and fouls are constantly being committed. The referee must have a quick eye and make fast judgments about which fouls should be

A water polo pool measures 82 feet by 66 feet (26 m by 20 m). The goal area is marked with colors on the side of the pool. The two-meter line is red, the four-meter line is yellow, the seven-meter line is green, and the goal line is white. There must be an area of at least one meter behind each goal line.

called. Because infractions are such a large part of the strategy of water polo, a referee employs what is known as the advantage rule. This is when a referee may refrain from calling a foul if he or she feels that making that call would give the advantage to the defense.

There are other officials in water polo who help the referee. There are two goal judges, one on each side of the pool. Their job is to indicate whether or not a goal has been scored. There are also two secretaries.

Their job is to manage the game clocks, to record all serious fouls committed by players, and to signal when a third exclusion or penalty foul has been made, in order to determine if a player needs to be removed from the game.

Since water polo is such a young sport and the rules have been modified so many times over the years, it is hard for referees to keep up. To deal with the problems that referees encounter, many countries have formed organizations for referees to help them perform their job. This is partly the result of complaints and threats from the Olympic committee to have the game erased from the Olympic program if the standards of refereeing do not improve. Standardized tests regarding the rules of the game and how to call fouls are issued to referees through these organizations. However, criticism of water polo referees is still common. Many believe that the quality of players and coaches has improved since the invention of the game but the quality of the referees has not.

To combat this problem, FINA offers a water polo referee school. The goal of the referee school is to increase the number as well as the quality of referees and to create uniform interpretations and applications of the rules of water polo. Only certified graduates of the FINA referee school may be selected for FINA-sanctioned competitions. Every two years, a FINA-certified referee must be re-examined and updated on changing rules in order to continue as a FINA water polo referee.

CHAPTER FOUR

The Players and Coaches

A water polo player tries to block a pass to an opponent. The light-colored and dark-colored caps make clear who's on which team.

Most water polo teams are made up of thirteen players, but only seven players from each team are allowed to be in the pool at one time, one of them being a goalkeeper. Team members who are sitting out the game must remain on the team bench and are not allowed to get up, except during a game interval. Because water polo is a game of thought and strategy as well as action, the positions of the players are important. Each player has a certain position in the pool when it comes to defense and offense. The positions of water polo are similar to those in basketball and soccer.

Drivers are similar to guards in basketball. Drivers

look for scoring opportunities for themselves and other team members. They specialize in driving skills, which include quick-shooting techniques, exceptional hand-eye coordination, and an extremely fast swimming technique. Drivers are mainly offensive players, but they are also involved in defensive play.

The center forward is another offensive player. A center forward positions himself or herself in front of the opponent's goal, between the two-meter and four-meter lines. This area is known as the hole. The center forward is sometimes called the hole man, and the shots that he or she takes are called hole shots. It's beneficial for the center forward to be a larger player. A center forward must have extraordinary leg strength and passing abilities. He or she must also be skilled at shot-taking, as he or she will be trying to score for most of the game. The position of center forward is similar to basketball's center position in that this player awaits a pass that will get him or her close to the goal for a shot. Center forwards are always heavily guarded by the defense.

More and more teams are starting to train utility players. Utility players have a position that is somewhat indefinable, as they play many roles in the water. Similar to halfbacks in soccer, utility players are both offensive and defensive players. They are the strongest shooters on the team and are in constant play, moving to

Although a water polo pool is usually too deep to do so, technically, a goalie can stand, jump from the floor of the pool, or walk. The goalie's main job is to make saves, but he or she can also score a goal.

wherever the ball may be, but mostly searching out opportunities to score goals.

The main line of defense in water polo is the two-meter defenders. The two-meter defenders are in charge of guarding the center forwards, or hole men. The most useful quality in a two-meter defender is agility, as he or she will have to constantly block passes. Most fouls are called on two-meter defenders, so they must be careful to commit no more than three and risk being removed from the game. The two-meter defender position is perhaps the most physically strenuous of all the positions in water polo. Most of the action is happening under the water, as the defender is usually pulling at the center forward, trying to hold him or her back from receiving passes or scoring. Two-meter defenders are the last line of defense before the goalies.

Goalies are the only players who are allowed to use both hands at once to handle the ball or to punch it with a closed fist, as long as they are within the four-meter line. The goalkeeper's main duty is to patrol the area between the goalposts and to make saves that will prevent scores. Goalies are not permitted to go beyond the center line, but they are allowed to take shots on an opponent's goal, so long as it's done from their half of the pool.

A goal is scored when the ball completely crosses the goal line. In order for a goal to be scored, two players must touch the ball after a start or restart, unless the team gets a penalty or free throw outside of seven meters.

The Coach

The techniques and physical demands of water polo are difficult to master and require an intense amount of training and organization. This is why the role of coaching is a crucial one. The duties of a water polo coach are far-reaching. Not only are they in charge of instructing their players, but they need to be effective team managers. A coach must coordinate swimming training, land conditioning (when a team trains out of the pool), ball skills, drills, and strategies. To do this, coaches must make use not only of athletic but also scientific, technical, and administrative resources. Many coaches study their craft through different manuals that are available from such organizations as the American Water Polo Coaches Association (AWPCA). With constant evolution of the drills and exercises employed to maximize a player's skills, coaches recognize that they need to stay current in order to lead their team to victory.

The AWPCA has an outlined code of ethics for water polo coaches. The AWPCA expects its coaches to have integrity. This means that it expects coaches to be honest and fair. It also asks for professional responsibility from coaches. But perhaps most important,

the AWPCA requests that coaches respect the officials and players, particularly the welfare of their players. Recognizing when players are sick or tired is the mark of a good coach. It is important for coaches and players to have a strong working relationship. The coach is essentially a member of the team, and as a team, the best road toward victory is to work together.

Because of the rigor and strength required of a water polo player, playing the game is obviously not for everybody, which may be the reason why the sport is not more popular. But participants in the sport are aware of this and are working to change it. Each year, the association USA Water Polo holds a meeting to discuss the future of the sport. Usually, the meetings are focused on the Olympics, but the association also works to promote interest in the sport on other amateur and professional levels.

However, almost anybody can enjoy being a spectator. Water polo was, after all, invented as a spectator sport. It is not that common to catch a water polo match on television but there are plenty of competitions and tournaments that take place on many levels, including high school, college, and international venues, and even local clubs.

The "Blood in the Water" Match

One of the most famous water polo matches in history took place during the 1956 Summer Olympics, held in Melbourne, Australia. As

There are specific rules for a coach's behavior. He or she can give instructions to the team but cannot shout continuously. The coach cannot pass the four meter area, and he or she is responsible for the behavior of all the players on the bench.

Unfair Advantage

Water polo players are extremely competitive and therefore will do anything to increase their performance in a game. Many players will shave their body hair to cut down on resistance in the water. Sometimes, players will try to put grease or oil on their bodies to increase their speed in the water. However, this action is illegal and is grounds for substitution.

the Hungarian athletes departed for Melbourne, a Soviet army, 200,000 strong, suppressed a smaller army of anti-communists in Budapest. Many of the Hungarian athletes were uncertain they would ever return home and said final farewells to loved ones.

The Soviet Union and Hungary then faced off in a semi-final water polo match in Melbourne. Many Hungarians who were then living in Australia filled the stands to cheer on their homeland team. News reports from Hungary had described the brutality the people were suffering under Soviet control. The Hungarian water polo team felt the only way to fight back was to beat the Soviet team.

Hungary's Deszo Gyarmati, who is considered by some experts today to be the greatest water polo player of all time, hit his Soviet defender when he scored the first goal. After Ervin Zador, another Hungarian star, scored two goals, he was pummeled by a Russian player. He suffered a deep gash under his right eye. The photo of the bleeding Zador was published in newspapers worldwide. The referee ended the match with less than a minute left. The pool had turned red with blood and there was fear the battle would spread to the stands. Hungary, however, won the match against the Soviets 4–0, then went on to win the championship by defeating Yugoslavia.

In June 2002, twelve players from both teams reunited in Budapest and reminisced about the bloody match. Zador, who was one of the twelve players to reunite, stated, "It should be clear that we never had any ill feelings toward the Russian people. It was just a match at the wrong time and the wrong place." One Russian player at the reunion confirmed that his team was also under immense pressure but confirmed that Hungary was the better team and would have won under any circumstances.

GLOSSARY

advantage rule The referee's option to not declare a foul, if it is his or her judgment that doing so would be an advantage to the offender's team. This ability speeds up the game and can result in more scoring.

brutality An exclusion foul that includes deliberately attacking an opponent or making any movements that are intended to endanger another player.

dribble To move and control the ball while swimming the crawl stroke.

drivers Field players who specialize in moving toward the goal and quick shooting techniques.

infraction A violation of rules.

interval A pause or break that takes place during a game. This happens in water polo in between quarters and at halftime.

pummel To beat with fists.

Trudgeon stroke A crawl variation with a scissors kick, named for J. Arthur Trudgeon, a famous British swimming instructor who was introduced to the swimming stroke in South America in the 1870s. In water polo, it enables quick passes, stops, starts, and turns.

FOR MORE INFORMATION

FINA World League
Av. De l'Avant—Poste 4
1005 Lausanne
Switzerland
Web site: http://fina.org

The National Collegiate Athletic Association (NCAA)
700 W. Washington Street
P.O. Box 6222
Indianapolis, IN 46206
Web site: http://www.ncaa.org

USA Water Polo National Office
1631 Mesa Avenue, Suite A-1
Colorado Springs, CO 80906

Web Sites

Due to the changing nature of Internet links, the Rosen Publishing Group, Inc., has developed an online list of Web sites related to the subject of this book. This site is updated regularly. Please use this link to access the list:

Http://www.rosenlinks.com/scc/wapo

FOR FURTHER READING

Anttila, William K. *Water Polo Drills and Playing Hints*. Palo Alto, CA: National Press, 1964.

Barr, David. *A Guide to Water Polo*. London: Museum Press, 1964.

Cutino, Pete. *101 Water Polo Defensive and Conditioning Drills*. Monterey, CA: Coaches Choice, 2001.

Hines, Charles. *How to Play and Teach Water Polo*. London: Kaye & Ward, 1969.

Juba, Kelvin. *All About Water Polo*. London: Pelham, 1972.

Kalbus, Barbara, ed. *2003-2004 NCAA Water Polo Rules*. Indianapolis, IN: National Collegiate Athletic Association, 2003.

Smith, James R. *The World Encyclopedia of Water Polo*. Los Olivos, CA: Olive Press Publications, 1989.

BIBLIOGRAPHY

De Mestre, Neville. *Water Polo: Techniques and Tactics.* Sydney, Australia: Angus and Robertson, 1972.

Hale, Ralph W., ed. *The Complete Book of Water Polo: The U.S. Olympic Water Polo Team's Manual for Conditioning, Strategy, Tactics, and Rules.* New York: Simon & Schuster, 1986.

Lambert, Arthur F. *The Technique of Water Polo: A Text for Player and Coach.* North Hollywood, CA: Swimming World, 1969.

Smith, James R. *Playing and Coaching Water Polo.* Los Angeles: W. F. Lewis, 1948.

INDEX

About the Author

Tracie Egan is a freelance writer who lives in Brooklyn, New York.

Photo Credits

Cover (left, right, group, and pool), pp. 1 (left and right), 3, 9 (inset), 14 (top and bottom), 16 (all four images), 17, 19 (all three images), 21 (all three images), 22, 23, 24, 26, 29 (top and bottom), 34, 36, 37, 38 © Robert Hudson and the Rosen Publishing Group; pp. 4 (top and bottom), 7, 8, 10, 12, 13 courtesy of International Swimming Hall of Fame; p. 9 © Petar Kujundzic/Reuters Newmedia Inc./Corbis; p. 17 (top) © Nelson Sá; pp. 32, 38 (inset) © Stan Liu/Icon SMI.

Thanks to Newport Harbor High School, Newport Beach, California.

Designer: Nelson Sá; **Editor:** Leigh Ann Cobb; **Photo Researcher:** Adriana Skura